Tennessee

By Kimberly Valzania

Consultant
Nanci R. Vargus, Ed.D.
Primary Multiage Teacher
Decatur Township Schools, Indianapolis, Indiana

Children's Press®
A Division of Scholastic Inc.
New York   Toronto   London   Auckland   Sydney
Mexico City   New Delhi   Hong Kong
Danbury, Connecticut

Designer: Herman Adler Design
Photo Researcher: Caroline Anderson
The photo on the cover shows the Newfound Gap, Great Smoky Mountains
National Park.

Library of Congress Cataloging-in-Publication Data

Valzania, Kim.
  Tennessee / by Kim Valzania.
      p. cm. — (Rookie read-about geography)
Includes index.
Summary: An introduction to Tennessee which focuses on the state's
geography.
  ISBN 0-516-22699-1 (lib. bdg.)   0-516-27843-6 (pbk.)
  1. Tennessee—Juvenile literature. 2. Tennessee—Geography—Juvenile
literature. [1. Tennessee.] I. Title. II. Series.
  F436.3 .V35 2003
  917.68—dc21   2002011556

JE
VAL
C. 1

$14.25

Where can you find a
waterfall that is under
the ground?

In the state of Tennessee!

Find Tennessee on this
map. It is shaped almost
like a rectangle.

CANADA

WASHINGTON

OREGON

IDAHO

MONTANA

NORTH DAKOTA

MINNESOTA

MICHIGAN

NEW HAMPSHIRE

VERMONT

MAINE

WYOMING

SOUTH DAKOTA

WISCONSIN

NEW YORK

MASSACHUSETTS

RHODE ISLAND

NEVADA

UTAH

COLORADO

NEBRASKA

IOWA

OHIO

PENNSYLVANIA

CONNECTICUT

NEW JERSEY

DELAWARE

ILLINOIS

INDIANA

WEST VIRGINIA

MARYLAND

CALIFORNIA

ARIZONA

KANSAS

MISSOURI

KENTUCKY

VIRGINIA

Washington, D.C.

NEW MEXICO

OKLAHOMA

ARKANSAS

TENNESSEE

NORTH CAROLINA

TEXAS

MISSISSIPPI

ALABAMA

GEORGIA

SOUTH CAROLINA

LOUISIANA

FLORIDA

ALASKA

CANADA

MEXICO

HAWAII

North

West   East

South

5

There are three parts to Tennessee. There is West, Middle, and East.

West Tennessee lies between the Mississippi River and the Tennessee River. It has hills, valleys (VAL-eez), and plains. The soil is very good for growing cotton.

8

West Tennessee has a large lake called Reelfoot Lake. The lake was formed in 1812 when an earthquake shook the ground.

Part of the forest sank. It filled with water from the Mississippi River!

Memphis is in West Tennessee. It is the biggest city in Tennessee.

Many people in Memphis work for companies that make medicines.

Middle Tennessee lies between two parts of the Tennessee River. The land dips down into the shape of a bowl. It is called a basin (BAY-suhn).

This part of the state has many caves and streams under the ground.

The land in Middle
Tennessee is just right
for raising farm animals.
Many cattle, hog, sheep,
and dairy farms can be
found there.

16

The largest city in Middle Tennessee is Nashville. Nashville is also the state capital.

Many people in Nashville work in the country music business.

Soybeans, tomatoes, cabbage, and apples are just a few of the crops grown in Middle Tennessee.

Cabbage

This area is also famous
for the Tennessee
Walking Horse.

Middle Tennessee has several large reservoirs (REZ-ur-vwarz). These are popular places for fishing.

A reservoir is a lake that is made by a dam. Dams are walls that hold back the flow of water.

East Tennessee begins
in the foothills of the
Appalachian (a-puh-LAY-
shee-uhn) Mountains.
The land is covered
in trees.

Visitors can see the
Cumberland Gap here.
Pioneers used to travel
through this gap.

Ruby Falls is in East Tennessee. It is a 145-foot waterfall.

This giant waterfall is special because it is inside a limestone cave. Visitors come from all around the world to see it.

Clingmans Dome

The Great Smoky Mountains are a major part of East Tennessee.

Some people like to hike and camp in the beautiful woods there. Some come to see Clingmans Dome. It is the highest point in Tennessee.

Which part of Tennessee
do you like best?

Words You Know

Cumberland Gap

Clingmans Dome

cotton

Memphis

30

Reelfoot Lake

reservoir

Ruby Falls

Tennessee Walking Horse

Index

Appalachian Mountains 23

caves 12, 24

Clingmans Dome 27, 30

cotton 6, 30

country music 17

Cumberland Gap 23, 30

farming 14, 18

Great Smoky Mountains 27

maps 4, 5, 13

Memphis 10, 30

Mississippi River 6, 9

Nashville (state capital) 17

Tennessee River 6, 12

Tennessee Walking Horse 19, 31

About the Author

Kimberly Valzania lives in Connecticut with her husband and two young children. She has worked as a freelance writer of educational books and materials for the past five years.

Photo Credits